Nova Scotia

Nova Scotia

Alexa Thompson

Lerner Publications Company

LIBRARY OF CONGRESS
CATALOGING-IN-PUBLICATION DATA

Thompson, Alexa.
    Nova Scotia / by Alexa Thompson.
        p. cm. — (Hello Canada)
    Includes index.
    ISBN 0–8225–2759–6 (lib. bdg.)
        1. Nova Scotia—Juvenile literature. [1. Nova Scotia.]
    I. Title. II. Series.
    F1037.4.T48 1995
    971.6—dc20   94–24101
                                        CIP
                                        AC

Cover photograph © James P. Rowan. Background photo by R. Chen/SuperStock.

The glossary on page 68 gives definitions of words shown in **bold type** in the text.

Senior Editor
Gretchen Bratvold
Editor
Colleen Sexton
Photo Researcher
Cindy Hartmon
Designer
Steve Foley

Our thanks to the following people for their help in preparing this book: Peter Kidd of Learning Materials Consulting Services, Halifax, and Vince Warner, a Maritime curriculum specialist from the Prince Edward Island Department of Education.

Manufactured in the United States of America
1 2 3 4 5 6 – JR – 00 99 98 97 96 95

 This book is printed on acid-free, recyclable paper.

Contents

Fun Facts

🍁 Nova Scotia has the world's highest tides. In the Bay of Fundy, tides can rise as high as 56 feet (17 meters). That's as tall as a five-storied building!

🍁 Canada's first newspaper was published in Nova Scotia. The debut issue of the *Halifax Gazette* came out in 1752, just three years after the city of Halifax was founded.

🍁 The fossilized bones of the world's tiniest dinosaur—the *coelurosaur*—can be found near the town of Parrsboro, Nova Scotia. No bigger than a chicken, these small creatures roamed the earth about 180 million years ago.

Hi! My name is Barkley. As you read *Nova Scotia*, I will be helping you make sense of some of the maps and charts that appear in the book.

🍁 Nova Scotia is nicknamed Land of Evangeline after the poem *Evangeline* by Henry Wadsworth Longfellow. The poem describes how, in 1755, the British forced early settlers called Acadians from their homes in Grand Pré.

🍁 About 1.5 million of the 5 million Christmas trees cut down in Canada every year come from Nova Scotia.

🍁 Nova Scotians are often called Bluenosers after the fishermen who work on the province's chilly coastal waters. The fishermen's noses, it is said, turn blue in the winter cold.

A statue of Evangeline, the heroine of the poem Evangeline, *stands in Grand Pré, Nova Scotia.*

A whale (above) **splashes in Nova Scotia's ocean waters. At Peggy's Cove, a lighthouse** (facing page) **is perched on a rocky shore.**

Canada's Ocean Playground

Surrounded on three sides by the waters of the Atlantic Ocean, Nova Scotia has hundreds of sandy beaches, deep bays, and jagged inlets. In fact, when you include the province's nearby islands, Nova Scotia's ragged coastline stretches a total of 4,709 miles (7,578 kilometers). With all this room for swimming, sailing, and fishing, it's no wonder that Nova Scotians call their province Canada's Ocean Playground.

No matter where you are in this eastern province, the sea is never more than 35 miles (56 km) away. The second smallest province in Canada, Nova Scotia covers slightly less area than the European country of Ireland. Together, Nova Scotia and its neighbors—New Brunswick and Prince Edward Island—are known as the Maritime Provinces. The Maritimes, along

On Cape Breton Island, small villages nestle among rugged shores and forested hills.

Swimmers and sunbathers (above) **crowd Nova Scotia's beaches during the summer. Fishing boats at the Bay of Fundy** (right) **wait for the tide to come in.**

with the province of Newfoundland to the northeast, make up Atlantic Canada.

Nova Scotia has two main parts—a mainland **peninsula,** which is almost completely surrounded by water, and Cape Breton Island. The Strait of Canso, a narrow but deep waterway, just barely separates the mainland from the island. People used to travel to and from the island by boat, but now they can drive across the Canso Causeway, the deepest **causeway** in the world.

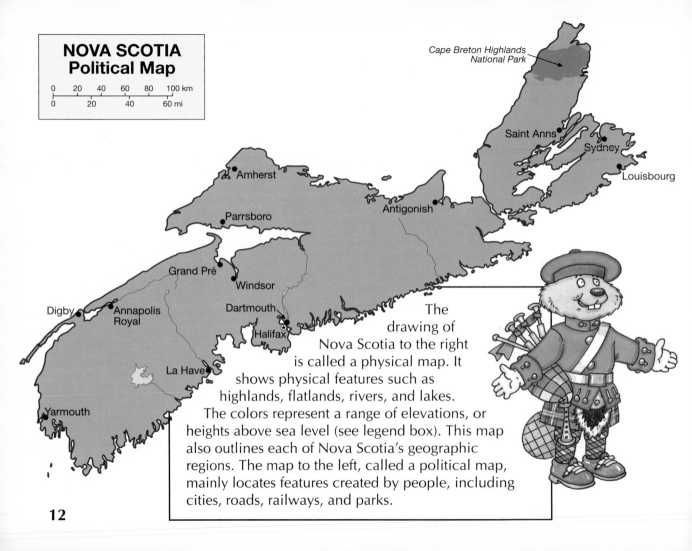

NOVA SCOTIA
Political Map

```
0    20   40   60   80   100 km
0        20       40        60 mi
```

Cape Breton Highlands
National Park

Saint Anns

Sydney

Louisbourg

Amherst

Antigonish

Parrsboro

Grand Pré

Windsor

Digby

Annapolis
Royal

Dartmouth

Halifax

La Have

Yarmouth

The drawing of Nova Scotia to the right is called a physical map. It shows physical features such as highlands, flatlands, rivers, and lakes. The colors represent a range of elevations, or heights above sea level (see legend box). This map also outlines each of Nova Scotia's geographic regions. The map to the left, called a political map, mainly locates features created by people, including cities, roads, railways, and parks.

12

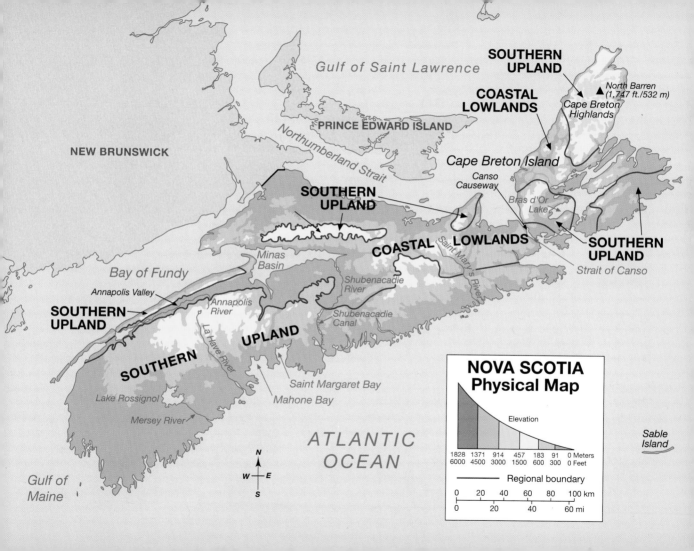

Gulf of Saint Lawrence

SOUTHERN UPLAND

COASTAL LOWLANDS

▲ North Barren
(1,747 ft./532 m)

Cape Breton
Highlands

PRINCE EDWARD ISLAND

NEW BRUNSWICK

Northumberland Strait

Cape Breton Island

Canso
Causeway

Bras d'Or
Lake

SOUTHERN UPLAND

COASTAL LOWLANDS

SOUTHERN UPLAND

Strait of Canso

Minas
Basin

Saint Mary's River

Bay of Fundy

Annapolis Valley

Annapolis
River

Shubenacadie
River

Shubenacadie
Canal

SOUTHERN UPLAND

SOUTHERN UPLAND

La Have River

Saint Margaret Bay

Mahone Bay

Lake Rossignol

Mersey River

ATLANTIC OCEAN

Gulf of Maine

N
W E
S

Sable
Island

NOVA SCOTIA
Physical Map

Elevation

| 1828 | 1371 | 914 | 457 | 183 | 91 | 0 Meters |
| 6000 | 4500 | 3000 | 1500 | 600 | 300 | 0 Feet |

―― Regional boundary

0   20   40   60   80   100 km

0   20   40   60 mi

About 3,800 small islands hug Nova Scotia's coast. The province also claims Sable Island, which is located far out in the Atlantic. Over the years, so many ships have sunk near Sable Island's shores that it has earned the nickname Graveyard of the Atlantic.

From the air, Nova Scotia looks a bit like the head of a hammer, stretching from the tip of Cape Breton Island in the northeast to Yarmouth, a port at the province's southwestern end. The hammer's neck is attached to New Brunswick, Nova Scotia's northwestern neighbor.

To the north, across the Northumberland Strait, the waters of the Gulf of Saint Lawrence cradle the province of Prince Edward Island. The Bay of Fundy separates southwestern Nova Scotia from New Brunswick, and the U.S. state of Maine lies to the west, just across the Gulf of Maine.

Many Nova Scotians get to Maine by taking a ferryboat across this small gulf, which is an arm of the Atlantic Ocean. The ferries—a common form of transportation in the Maritimes—carry passengers and their cars to and from ports in Nova Scotia, New Brunswick, and Prince Edward Island.

Sometimes Nova Scotia's unpredictable weather can make ferry crossings difficult. Storms and high winds batter the province, especially in fall and winter. About 53 inches (135 centimeters) of rain and snow fall in the province each year. In winter sea ice lines the coast until late March.

The climate of Nova Scotia and the rest of Atlantic Canada is affected by two sea currents—the Labrador Current

Workers scrape winter snow and ice from the deck of a boat.

and the Gulf Stream. Flowing northward from the Gulf of Mexico, the Gulf Stream carries warm water to the region. The Labrador Current sweeps down from the north, bringing ice-cold water from the Arctic Ocean.

Together, these currents bring mild temperatures to Nova Scotia. Winters aren't as cold and summers aren't as hot in the province as in other parts of Canada. In July the province's temperature averages 64° F (18° C), while average readings for January dip to 23° F (–5° C). In summer the cold sea chills the warm, damp air, often creating a thick fog along the coast.

15

A wave crashes against the rough shore of the Southern Upland.

Thousands of years ago, the climate was much colder in the Maritime region. **Glaciers**—enormous sheets of ice—crept southward across Nova Scotia, scraping the land, grinding boulders and plants into the soil, rounding off mountain peaks, and gouging out valleys. The last of these glaciers melted about 12,000 years ago.

Nova Scotia's land continues to change. The whole province was once a vast plain called the Atlantic Upland, but it can now be divided into three regions. The province's Southern Upland, on the southern half of the mainland, is a large slice of the old Atlantic Upland. Over thousands of years, glaciers, rivers, wind, and other natural forces wore down areas of the Atlantic Upland that were made of soft rock and loose soil. Primarily on the northern half of the mainland, these low-lying areas now form the fertile Coastal Lowlands. Cape Breton Island can be considered the third land region in Nova Scotia.

In the Southern Upland, rolling hills covered with thick pine and birch forests stretch across the landscape. White-tailed deer, wildcats, beavers, minks, squirrels,

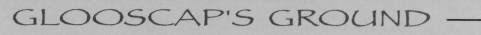

GLOOSCAP'S GROUND

According to Micmac legend, a mighty spirit named Glooscap once ruled the lands bordering the Bay of Fundy. Glooscap, who had magical powers, shaped the jagged coastline and controlled the strong ocean tides. The spirit also scattered sparkling stones—jasper, agate, amethyst, and onyx—along the shores and threw clumps of dirt into the sea to make small islands. The ancient Micmacs believed that Glooscap made this land into one of the most beautiful places on earth.

raccoon, and red foxes make their homes in these wooded areas. And residents of this region are never surprised to see a moose or a black bear passing through their backyards!

Much of the coast of the Southern Upland is barren and rocky. Glaciers gouged out several large inlets, including Saint Margaret Bay and Mahone Bay. Many residents along the southern shore make a living from the sea, fishing for lobsters, scallops, crabs, clams, pollack, and haddock.

Halifax, the province's capital and largest city, lies midway along the southern coast. A deep, narrow harbor protects this busy port city from storms and sea ice. Bridges and passenger ferries link Halifax to the neighboring community of Dartmouth. About one-third of all Nova Scotians live in the Halifax-Dartmouth area.

The star-shaped Halifax Citadel—a historic military fort—overlooks Halifax. The residents of this capital city are called Haligonians.

From Dartmouth, the Shubenacadie Canal joins a chain of lakes with the Shubenacadie River. This waterway flows northward to the Minas Basin, which is part of the Bay of Fundy. Other important rivers in the Southern Upland include the Saint Mary's and the La Have. The Mersey River flows through Lake Rossignol, the biggest of many lakes in the region.

The Coastal Lowlands spread across the northern half of the mainland. Rolling farmland, long stretches of sandy beaches, and **marshes** (grassy wetlands) are all found in the region. Beneath the ground lie rich deposits of minerals such as coal and gypsum.

In the spring, colorful wildflowers, including wild iris, violets, and pitcher plants, decorate the hillsides of the Coastal Lowlands. One of the most beautiful plants is the trailing arbutus, or mayflower, the province's official flower. In small wooded areas, deer and porcupines are common. Ducks, grebes, blue herons, loons, and piping plovers feed on marshland plants, including mosses, lichens, and ferns. Bog laurel, tamarack, and alder also grow in the marshlands.

The Annapolis River Valley in the western Coastal Lowlands is famous for its apple orchards. Farms in this area also produce corn, potatoes, beans, squash, and pumpkins. In the central section of the Coastal Lowlands, farmers raise dairy cattle and plant small vegetable plots.

A porcupine (above) *searches for food. Porcupines like to climb to the tops of pines to eat the trees' sweet tips. Lupines* (below) *color Nova Scotia's fields in the summer.*

Thick fog blankets the rolling hills of the Coastal Lowlands.

Three patches of the old Atlantic Upland jut up from the Coastal Lowlands. Steep cliffs drop down to the Bay of Fundy in the northwest and to the Gulf of Saint Lawrence in the northeast. In the northern mainland, the flat-topped Cobequid Mountains rise nearly 1,000 feet (300 m).

Uplands and lowlands form a patchwork across Cape Breton Island.

The Cape Breton Highlands, a low mountain range, run across the northern part of the island. Here the North Barren Mountain rises 1,747 feet (532 m)—the highest point in Nova Scotia. Thick forests of pine and fir trees cover the island's uplands.

Bras d'Or Lake nearly cuts Cape Breton Island in half. From openings to the Atlantic Ocean, small seagoing boats can travel across this huge salt-water lake to the middle of the island. Visitors crowd the lake's beaches during the summer to sail, swim, or fish for Atlantic salmon.

About one-fifth of Nova Scotia's population lives on Cape Breton Island. Most of the island's residents—called Capers—make their homes in and around Sydney, an important industrial city. Nearby mining towns provide coal to Sydney's steel mill. Coal also is used to produce much of Nova Scotia's electrical power. Trains transport products made on Cape Breton Island across the Canso Causeway to inland destinations.

A brook rushes between bright, autumn-colored trees on Cape Breton Island.

Micmacs and Colonists

The first people known to have set foot in what is now Nova Scotia were Paleo-Indians, who reached the Maritime region about 11,000 years ago. These groups survived by hunting caribou for food. But when the large herds began to dwindle, the Paleo-Indians left the area.

By about 5500 B.C., Maritime Archaic Indians had moved into the region to fish the coastal waters and to hunt seals, walrus, and other large sea mammals. These groups also trapped small game animals and gathered berries and other food plants from the forests.

About 2,500 years ago, the Micmac Indians, who may have descended from the Maritime Archaic Indians, settled in what is now Nova Scotia. The Micmacs were expert craftspeople. They dyed porcupine quills and used the colorful shafts in patterns on clothing and containers. From birch trees, these Native peoples shaped long, sturdy canoes and built frames for wigwams (cone-shaped dwellings covered with animal skins).

In winter the Micmacs hunted in small bands, tracking deer, moose, and other game through inland forests. Several bands joined together during the spring and summer, when they moved their camps to the coast. Here the Micmacs fished and dried their catch in the sun before storing it for the winter. Fall was the time to gather berries and to sew animal skins into warm winter clothing.

The Micmacs were probably one of the first Native groups in what is now Canada to come in contact with Europeans. About A.D. 1000, Norse adventurers sailed westward from Greenland and may have landed on what is now Nova Scotia. The Norse traveled the coastal waters and explored the shoreline.

In 1497 John Cabot, an Italian explorer working for the king of England, landed on the southern mainland and sailed up the coast to Cape Breton Island. He claimed all of the land he had explored for the English king. When Cabot returned to England, he told stories about a sea so full of fish that you could easily catch one just by dipping your hand in the water.

In summer the Micmacs camped on Nova Scotia's ocean shores and used birchbark canoes to travel along the coast.

In 1497 explorer John Cabot landed on what is now Cape Breton Island and claimed the territory for England.

Cabot's stories excited European fishermen. Crews from England, Ireland, France, Portugal, and Spain followed Cabot's route. They spent their summers hauling in cod from the North Atlantic Ocean. Some fishing crews pitched summer camps on Cape Breton Island, where they met the Micmacs. The Indians gave the newcomers furs in exchange for blankets and tools.

More and more French fishermen came after Jacques Cartier explored the region for France in 1534. Cartier claimed all the land that he saw—including what is now Nova Scotia—for France. Over time, the French came to call this area *L'Acadie,* or Acadia. It included almost the entire southeastern coast of what is now Canada plus part of the present-day state of Maine.

Although both England and France claimed the same territory, neither nation was ready to set up a permanent settlement. They were more interested in shipping the region's valuable resources back to Europe. While the French concentrated on fishing, the English focused on the fur trade.

By the early 1600s, however, the French king Henry IV was eager to take control of the fur industry and the fishing business in the Maritime region. To help establish French fur traders here, the king gave Pierre du Gua de Monts the right to set up a permanent **colony,** which would be ruled by faraway France.

In 1604 de Monts, explorer Samuel de Champlain, and more than 70 other men set up a camp in Acadia. Half of the colonists became ill and didn't survive the first winter. Without the help of the Micmacs, who gave the French settlers food, firewood, and furs, the rest would have died, too. In the spring, the remaining colonists chose a new site, which they called Port Royal.

At Port Royal, the newcomers fished, planted crops, and trapped animals for their furs. But the colonists couldn't survive without supplies from France. So, many of the men left for the winters and returned in the summers. After three years, the king decided to take away de Monts's rights to the colony. Without the government's help, Port Royal's residents could not survive, and they all returned to France.

Some of these original settlers later came back to Acadia to try to set up new colonies with other French farmers and their families. These newcomers, who over time became known as Acadians, found fertile but marshy land that disappeared beneath the sea at high tide. The Acadians built **dikes** (barriers) to keep the sea from flooding the rich soil. Old and young people alike worked to maintain these earthen walls that protected fields of wheat, rye, and corn.

By the mid-1600s, about 70 families had settled in Acadia, mainly in Port Royal. They built their houses on hills that overlooked the croplands. To get supplies they couldn't make, the Acadians traded with New Englanders in the more established English colonies to the south.

Although they traded with the Acadians, the English worried about a growing Acadian population. To keep control of fishing and the fur trade in the region, England fought France throughout the 1600s. Between 1604 and 1710, the countries tossed control of Acadia back and forth nine times.

In 1713 the French lost control of all of Acadia except Cape Breton Island and Ile Saint Jean (now Prince Edward Island). By this time, England had formed the United Kingdom of Great Britain and ruled territories in many areas of the world. Under British rule, the rest of Acadia became known as Nova Scotia, meaning New Scotland.

Many Acadians continued to live under British rule at Port Royal, which the British had renamed Annapolis Royal. As the Acadian population

Acadian farmers harvested hay and other crops in the rich soil of eastern Nova Scotia. To keep the ocean from flooding their fields, the Acadians built earthen walls called dikes (background).

grew, farmers looking for new land built settlements at Grand Pré and Beaubassin (present-day Amherst) to the north and at La Have to the south.

Some Acadians moved to Cape Breton Island, which had become a French colony. French soldiers built the colony's capital, Louisbourg, on the eastern shore. Settlers fished for cod to sell overseas and sold supplies to ships that docked at the colony's port. To protect these settlers from the British, French soldiers built a tall, stone fortress around Louisbourg, making the city a key military outpost.

As with Annapolis Royal, ownership of Louisbourg shifted back and forth between the French and the British. To create a British stronghold in Nova Scotia, the British built their own fort at Halifax in 1749 and made the port their capital.

Far removed from this new British outpost, the Acadians and Micmacs in and around Annapolis Royal lived side by side. Angry with the British for invading Indian hunting grounds, the Micmacs helped the French in their struggle with the British for control of the Maritime region. The Micmacs attacked British posts and ships.

Although worried about Native loyalites, the British were more concerned that French-speaking Acadians would rebel against British rule. In 1755 the British governor of Nova Scotia, Charles Lawrence, demanded that the

Warships and trading vessels anchored in Louisbourg's harbor in the mid-1700s. Louisbourg's huge stone fortress made the port an important military base during the Seven Years' War.

Acadians take an oath of loyalty to the British king. Lawrence ordered British soldiers to drive out all settlers who refused.

The Acadians called this time the *Grand Dérangement,* or the Great Upheaval. British soldiers traveled from village to village, forcing Acadians onto transport ships and burning their homes and farms. Families were separated and sent to different areas of the world, including France, Québec, New England, and the French colony of Louisiana (in what is now the state of Louisiana). In all, the British uprooted about 6,000 Acadians.

The struggle for the Maritime territories finally ended in 1758, when the British defeated the French at Louisbourg. This battle was part of the Seven Years' War, which raged between the

British soldiers set fire to Acadian homes during the Great Upheaval, a time when the British forced the Acadians out of Nova Scotia.

French and the British both in Europe and North America. In 1759 French rule was toppled forever in all of the territories that eventually became part of Canada.

The Best of Times and the Worst of Times

The end of the Seven Years' War brought change to the Maritime region. In the 1760s, thousands of New Englanders traveled to Nova Scotia. They built new settlements on some of the farmland that had once belonged to Acadians. Many **immigrants** also came from England, Scotland, Ireland, Germany, and Switzerland. And some Acadians returned to farm the marshlands.

After 1775 settlers in 13 of the British colonies to the south of Nova Scotia gained independence from British rule. These colonists formed a new country called the United States. Thousands of people were still loyal to Britain, however. So they moved north to Nova Scotia and to other British colonies. Called **Loyalists,** these people included black slaves seeking freedom.

A group of Loyalists arrives in Nova Scotia in the 1770s. The Loyalists were colonists from the newly formed United States who were still loyal to Britain.

Many Loyalists, along with a large number of Scottish immigrants, settled on Cape Breton Island to farm and to fish. By the early 1800s, people were arriving in Nova Scotia daily from the United States and from Europe to begin new lives. Many settlers made their homes in farming communities and built churches and schools. To help govern its territories more efficiently, Britain made Cape Breton Island part of Nova Scotia in 1820.

Some newcomers moved to Halifax, a bustling seaport. Dockworkers unloaded manufactured goods from Europe. Ships heading back to Europe

Shipbuilding was a big business in Nova Scotia during the 1800s.

carried raw materials, including timber from Nova Scotia's forests. Local shipbuilders used some of the timber to build the ships that carried goods overseas. Soon Nova Scotia had one of the largest shipping fleets in the world.

In smaller shipyards throughout the province, workers built boats to support the thriving fishery. Fishermen sailed to fertile fishing areas on large ships called schooners, which carried rowboats. Crew members fished from the small boats and then returned to the schooners to salt their catch. Salting preserved the fish until it could be sold in local markets.

While shipping, trading, and fishing were booming, a newspaper publisher and politician named Joseph Howe was working to change the way Nova Scotia was governed. At that time, a

Joseph Howe

British governor ran the colony and made all the laws. The governor received advice from members of the Nova Scotia Assembly, an elected group of citizens. But the members didn't have any real power. The governor made the final decisions.

35

These miners worked at the underground coal mines on Cape Breton Island.

Joseph Howe argued that Nova Scotians should be free to choose their own government officials and to make their own laws. Finally, Britain agreed. In 1848 Britain gave Nova Scotia **responsible government**—a government elected by the people to create and enforce local laws.

In Nova Scotia and in other British colonies, politicians began to talk about uniting under one government. After three years of debate, Ontario, Québec, New Brunswick, and Nova Scotia united to form a new country called the Dominion of Canada. **Confederation,** or the official union of these colonies, took place on July 1, 1867.

Under the terms of Confederation, workers paid by the Canadian government built the Intercolonial Railway. Trade in the region increased as trains carried immigrants and goods that arrived by ship in Nova Scotia to Ontario and Québec. The railroad provided jobs for many Nova Scotians, and towns sprang up alongside the train tracks.

Throughout the late 1800s and early 1900s, Canadian railroads used a lot of Nova Scotia's coal. Workers dug the coal from mines on the northern mainland and near Sydney on Cape Breton Island. A booming industrial town, Sydney also produced steel—a strong metal made from iron ore, coal, and other minerals. At Sydney's steel mill, laborers manufactured rails for railways and sheets of metal for ships.

The demand for steel rose even more during World War I (1914–1918), when Canada's navy needed more ships. Because Nova Scotia was a center for trade and shipbuilding, the province served as an international naval headquarters. Fleets sailed from Halifax to deliver troops, weapons, food, and supplies to Europe, where most of the fighting took place.

The Halifax Explosion

During World War I, naval ships from many countries stopped in Halifax Harbor to pick up troops and supplies. On the foggy morning of December 6, 1917, two ships collided in the harbor. The *Mont Blanc*—a French ship carrying explosives—burst into flames when it hit a cargo ship. Then, at exactly 9:05 A.M., the *Mont Blanc* blew up.

The huge explosion killed 2,000 people and injured another 8,000. Much of the north end of Halifax was leveled. It took many years for Halifax to be rebuilt. But slowly, one by one, workers reconstructed damaged buildings.

Nowadays, every December 6 at 9:05 A.M., residents of Halifax gather beneath memorial bells in a park overlooking the harbor. Here, they remember the people who died in the explosion and those who helped rebuild the city.

A drilling rig in Halifax Harbor taps oil from beneath the ocean floor.

After the war, hard times fell on Nova Scotia. During the 1930s—a period known as the Great Depression—mines, fisheries, banks, and businesses closed. Thousands of Nova Scotians lost their jobs.

World War II (1939–1945) boosted Nova Scotia's economy. Docks in Halifax again bustled with activity as ships loaded with weapons, troops, and supplies headed for war-torn western Europe. In the 1950s, the province was able to use some of the money it had earned during the war to build new schools and highways.

But on Cape Breton Island, coal supplies began to run out, and some of the steel operations in Sydney shut down. Many shipbuilders in the province also lost their jobs as the demand for wooden ships dropped.

Since then the government has tried to set up new industries in Nova Scotia. In the fishery, for example, big processing plants built in the 1950s and 1960s provided new jobs. Here workers began making fish fillets and freezing them for transport to faraway markets. But competition from countries in other areas of the world has grown, and the numbers of fish in the North Atlantic Ocean have dropped. With fewer fish, many Nova Scotian fishers and processing workers face hard times.

In mining towns and in coastal fishing villages throughout Nova Scotia, many people have lost their jobs. Young people who can't find work are moving west to other provinces where they may have better luck.

In recent years, industries such as paper milling and tire manufacturing have started up. More ships are docking in Nova Scotia, especially in Halifax where new container ship terminals were built. And the tourism industry also has picked up as more advertising has attracted visitors to the province's beautiful beaches and forests.

Nova Scotia's economy still lags behind those of the bigger industrial provinces to the west. But Nova Scotia's future is looking brighter. New coal mines on Cape Breton Island are sending some workers back to the mines. Scientists have also found oil and natural gas beneath the ocean floor. Tapping these resources will soon put more Nova Scotians to work.

Fish and the Future

For hundreds of years, Nova Scotians have depended on fish, forests, and minerals to make a living. For awhile these natural resources were plentiful. But Nova Scotians have learned that fish, trees, and coal can disappear quickly without careful management.

Some of Nova Scotia's **primary resources** are almost used up. Many residents have been forced to look for jobs in industries that don't rely on natural resources. But because Nova Scotia is far from central Canada—the economic center of the nation—the province has had trouble attracting new businesses. And many of these new industries have not survived. So many workers continue to rely on Nova Scotia's limited natural resources to make a living.

A fisher (facing page) *unloads his catch at the wharf of a fish-processing plant. A stack of lobster traps* (above) *lines a dock.*

The fishery has been a way of life in Nova Scotia since Europeans first sailed across the Atlantic Ocean to the province's shores. Up until the 1980s, the industry thrived. Huge boats called factory trawlers scooped up tons of fish—especially cod—which were processed into fishburgers and other seafood products right on board. Other fishers hauled their catch to processing plants on shore.

By the late 1980s, however, the number of cod and other groundfish (fish that feed at the bottom of the ocean) had dropped drastically. Experts aren't sure why the fish are disappearing. Some blame trawlers for overfishing. Others think an increased number of seals are eating the fish. A few scientists blame a slight drop in the temperature of the Atlantic Ocean.

The cold may have sent the fish swimming farther south, where ocean temperatures are warmer.

The decline of the fishery has affected entire coastal communities in Nova Scotia. Processing plants have closed, and many families have left the province. Some people who worked in the fishery are going back to school to learn new job skills. Others are hoping the fish will return.

In the meantime, the Canadian government is taking steps to help the fishery. In 1994 officials banned cod fishing in Canada's North Atlantic waters, hoping that the cod would then survive and multiply. The government also sends out patrol boats to make sure fishers from other countries aren't overfishing in Canadian waters. Although cod was the most important

Harvested logs float down a river near Digby, a major lumber center in Nova Scotia.

catch, Nova Scotia's fishers still make a living netting lobsters, scallops, mussels, and herring. The fishery employs only about 3 percent of Nova Scotia's workers, but the industry earns a lot of money.

Since the early days of shipbuilding, forestry has been an important industry in Nova Scotia. About three-fourths of the province's land is covered with trees, yet only 1 percent of workers hold jobs in forestry. Most of the trees in Nova Scotia are firs, such as spruce and balsam, which are used to make paper. Others are cut down for Christmas trees. Nova Scotians realize that the forestry industry won't survive if loggers chop down all the trees. For this reason, laws require logging companies to plant a tree for each one that they cut down.

Cows on a dairy farm near Truro graze on fertile fields.

Farms in the Annapolis Valley and in northern Nova Scotia occupy about one-tenth of the province's land. Some fruits and vegetables are grown, but the largest agricultural industry is dairying. Cows provide milk, some of which is made into butter and cheese. Farmers, who make up 2 percent of the province's workforce, also raise chickens, turkeys, hogs, and beef cattle.

Mining employs another 1 percent of Nova Scotia's workers. Miners dig up gypsum, sand, gravel, and other materials used by construction crews. But the most important mineral is coal, most of which is mined on Cape Breton Island. Coal provides about 70 percent of the fuel needed to generate electricity in Nova Scotia. But smoke from burning coal can pollute the air. So power stations carefully monitor the air quality and use filters in smokestacks to absorb some of the pollution before it enters the air.

Homegrown Harvest

Some farmers in Nova Scotia are subsistence farmers. This means that they grow enough food to feed their families year-round. Take Marlene and Don, for example. Their small farm is near the village of New Germany in southwestern Nova Scotia.

Most of their farmland is one large field where a horse grazes freely. Marlene and Don also have a nanny goat and her kid. The goat provides milk, and the kid will be slaughtered for meat. They raise other farm animals, too. About 15 hens roost in the barn. Marlene collects eggs from 5 of the hens every day, while the other 10 are fattened up for the dinner table. The family also keeps rabbits, some of which they sell to a nearby pet store. In the yard, 4 ducks swim in an old bathtub that has been sunk into the ground. Duck eggs, Marlene says, are great for making cakes.

In the garden beside the house, Marlene grows corn, beets, turnips, carrots, and potatoes. The root vegatables, such as turnips and potatoes, will be stored in the cool root cellar beneath the house. Marlene freezes or cans the other vegetables for the winter.

In the mornings, Don goes fishing at a local lake. During the deer-hunting season, he heads off to the woods. Don also spends time on the farm, mending fences and doing other odd jobs.

Subsistence farming is a hard life. Marlene and Don are often up before 5 A.M. to feed the animals and to clean the barn. And they seldom get to bed before midnight, after all the chores are done.

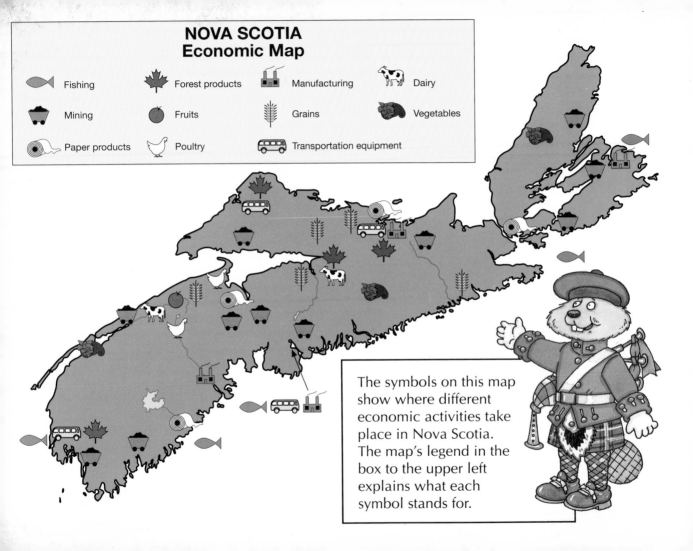

NOVA SCOTIA
Economic Map

Fishing

Forest products

Manufacturing

Dairy

Mining

Fruits

Grains

Vegetables

Paper products

Poultry

Transportation equipment

The symbols on this map show where different economic activities take place in Nova Scotia. The map's legend in the box to the upper left explains what each symbol stands for.

At refineries workers process oil into gasoline and other products. Ships bring oil from all over the world to be refined in Nova Scotia. And some oil is drilled from a site near Sable Island. Exploration crews at Sable Island have also found natural gas beneath the ocean floor. Nova Scotians hope that natural gas will soon flow through pipelines to the mainland.

Most of Nova Scotia's factories make products from the province's natural resources. At food-processing plants, workers grind fish and package it for sale. Mills process trees into wood pulp for paper. But not all manufacturers in Nova Scotia depend on natural resources. Laborers also assemble cars and develop new computer technologies. About 11 percent of Nova Scotia's workforce hold jobs in manufacturing.

The Annapolis Tidal Generating Station is the first plant in North America to use ocean tides to make electricity. Engineers have built a barrier called a dam across the Annapolis River near the spot where it meets the Bay of Fundy. As the tide rises, water pressure builds up against the dam and opens gates in the dam's walls. When a large area on the other side of the dam—called a head pond—is full of water, the gates close.

Later, when the tide is heading out to sea, workers open the dam's gates, and water flows back toward the Bay of Fundy. As the water rushes back through the dam, it turns the blades of a huge wheel, called a turbine. The turbine drives a machine called a generator, which produces electricity.

Since they come and go every six hours, the tides provide an unending source of energy. And unlike electricity generated by burning coal or natural gas, the power station at Annapolis Royal doesn't pollute the air.

Most working Nova Scotians—77 percent—have service jobs. Service workers help people or other businesses. Bankers, teachers, doctors, and politicians all have service jobs.

Transportation is a big service industry in Nova Scotia. Cruise ships bring tourists to the province, and huge cargo ships with decks longer than a football field often dock in Halifax.

Cranes unload huge containers full of goods from a ship.

A guide at the Fortress of Louisbourg—a historic site on Cape Breton Island—shows off his sword.

Workers operate cranes that hoist huge containers full of everything from cars to clocks off the ships and onto trains and semitrailer trucks. From Halifax the containers are transported across Canada.

With its sandy beaches, small fishing villages, and historic sites, Nova Scotia has a thriving tourism industry. The Fortress of Louisbourg, the Halifax Citadel, and the lighthouse at Peggy's Cove are just a few of the attractions that bring more than one million visitors to the province every year. Many Nova Scotians in the tourism industry work as travel agents, tour guides, innkeepers, waiters, or deep-sea fishing guides.

Many Cultures, One Community

Nova Scotia is home to more than 900,000 people from many different backgrounds. About half of all Nova Scotians live in small coastal towns or in the countryside. The rest make their homes in cities, including the Halifax-Dartmouth area and Sydney.

About 80 percent of Nova Scotians have ancestors who came from Europe—mainly from Britain. Of these, about 30 percent claim a Scottish heritage. Their ancestors, who thought Nova Scotia looked a lot like Scotland, brought many traditions to their new homeland. A few residents of Scottish descent still speak Gaelic, the traditional language of the Highland Scots.

A fisher casts a line into a stream (facing page). *Restaurants, shops, and museums bring crowds to the Halifax waterfront* (below). *Strawberry picking* (right) *is a fun outing in the countryside.*

Dressed in colorful kilts, two girls perform a traditional Scottish dance.

Nearly every weekend, Scots gather to celebrate their heritage. The biggest festivals include the Highland Games in Antigonish and the Nova Scotia Gaelic Mod in Saint Anns. The sounds of bagpipes and fiddles fill the air as dancers step in time to the music. On these occasions, many people dress in kilts—pleated skirts in plaid patterns called **tartans**. At one event, contestants show their strength by tossing end over end a wooden pole called a caber that is the size of a telephone pole.

About 11 percent of Nova Scotians are descendants of the Acadians. Many Acadians live either on the northeastern coast of Cape Breton Island or on the western mainland near Yarmouth and Digby. Not many Acadians farm anymore. In the early and mid-1900s, Acadians along the coast found work in

At the historic Acadian village of Grand Pré, women join in a quilting bee (above). *An Acadian fisher* (right) *repairs his nets.*

the fishery. Nowadays Acadians hold all kinds of jobs. They work as doctors, truck drivers, and teachers.

Most Acadians speak French and send their children to French-speaking schools. Many others preserve their past through music, art, and literature. Folklorists, for example, perform Acadian songs and tell stories to eager crowds. Artists paint scenes from the daily lives of both early and modern Acadians. And poets and novelists have found a large audience for their descriptions of traditional Acadian life.

A boy displays his catch—a snapping crab.

Nova Scotia is home to the nation's oldest African Canadian community, whose ancestors escaped from slavery in the United States during the 1700s and 1800s. Black Nova Scotians make up about 2 percent of the province's population. Most live either in the north end of Halifax or in the Prestons, just outside of Dartmouth. Proud of their heritage, members of the black community opened the Black Cultural Centre in Westphal to celebrate the history and the contributions of blacks to Canadian life.

Although the first black people to come to Nova Scotia found freedom, their descendants often have faced discrimination, or unfair treatment because of their color. When the economy is in a slump, blacks are sometimes the last to be hired. Those who do find work generally earn less money than most other Nova Scotians. To overcome these problems, Nova Scotians are working together to provide more opportunities for blacks.

Micmac Indians make up less than 1 percent of Nova Scotia's population. Most Micmacs live on the province's

13 **reserves**—land set aside by the government for Native peoples. Some Indians run small businesses on the reserves and continue to hunt, fish, and make traditional crafts. Micmacs at the Eskasoni reserve on Cape Breton Island run their own schools. But many Micmacs have no work, and poor housing conditions on the reserves add to an already hard life.

Some Native peoples have moved to the cities to learn new job skills and to look for work. The Micmac Native Friendship Centre in Halifax provides social and educational services to city-dwelling Native peoples.

A Micmac family dances at a powwow on Cape Breton Island.

Like black Nova Scotians, Micmacs have suffered from discrimination for a long time. But many Micmacs are working to help Nova Scotians recognize that Micmac heritage is valuable and important.

Nova Scotians of all backgrounds—including immigrants from eastern

Cooks (left) **grill up some tasty food at the Muliticultural Festival in Halifax. Jugglers on stilts** (above) **perform at a park on the Halifax waterfront.**

Europe, Asia, and Africa—celebrate their heritage at the annual Multicultural Festival on the Dartmouth waterfront. Here residents try ethnic foods that range from spicy Italian sausages to tasty Indian curries.

Other popular events in Nova Scotia include the Grand Prix Auto Race and the Annapolis Valley Apple Blossom Festival, which features barbecues, fireworks, and concerts. In Halifax the Nova Scotia International Tattoo presents musicians, comedians, singers, and dancers from around the world.

Nova Scotia's cities offer a variety of arts and entertainment. With a combined population of about 300,000 people, the Halifax-Dartmouth metropolitan area makes up Canada's largest urban center east of Montréal. Residents and vacationers enjoy visit-

Many Nova Scotians eat lobster, crab, mussels, and other delicious seafood caught in the province's coastal waters.

ing art galleries. History buffs tour the province's museums, such as the Marine Museum of the Atlantic, which displays many types of ships.

In summer Nova Scotians head for the beach to swim and soak up the sun. On lazy summer afternoons, sunbathers watch windsurfers dart across the waves. Sailing races also draw many fans to Nova Scotia's shores.

Good weather sends Nova Scotians hiking through inland forests or canoeing and fishing on lakes and streams. A favorite spot for nature lovers is Cape Breton Highlands National Park. In the province's marshes, wildlife **sanctuaries** shelter ducks, grebes, blue herons, bald eagles, ospreys, and loons. Some forestry companies invite visitors to walk along their nature trails, observe the animals, and learn about forest management.

Many Nova Scotians will tell you that they suffer from cabin fever in winter. Cabin fever is that restless feeling you get when you've been stuck indoors for too long on cold, snowy days. When cabin fever strikes, residents bundle up and head outdoors to down-hill ski, cross-country ski, or snowshoe over the drifts.

Many people like to ice fish in winter, dangling a hook and line through a hole drilled in the ice. And lots of Nova Scotians play ice hockey. Although there are indoor ice arenas, many hockey enthusiasts enjoy clearing a patch of ice on a frozen lake, lacing on their skates, and passing the puck outdoors. No matter what the season, Nova Scotians take full advantage of their beautiful surroundings.

Nova Scotians enjoy a wide variety of outdoor activities, including surfing (facing page left), *skiing* (facing page right), *and biking* (right).

Famous Nova Scotians

■ **Charles Bruce** (1906–1971), an author and a journalist, was born in Port Shoreham, Nova Scotia. Bruce worked for the news agency Canadian Press for 35 years. His best known book is *The Mulgrave Road,* for which he won the Governor General's Award.

2 **Ernest Buckler** (1908–1984), born in Dalhousie West, Nova Scotia, was a novelist who wrote about his native Annapolis Valley. Buckler's works include *The Mountain and the Valley, Nova Scotia: Window on the Sea,* and *Whirligig.*

3 **Holly Cole** (born 1964) formed a jazz group called the Holly Cole Trio in the late 1980s. Their recordings include "Calling You" and "Girl Talk." The trio's sold-out performances in Canada, the United States, and Japan have won rave reviews. Cole is a native of Halifax.

4 **Alex Colville** (born 1920), an artist, has shown his paintings in North America, Europe, and Asia. His subjects include his family, his animals, and the landscape near his home. Colville, who lives in Wolfville, Nova Scotia, also has served as chancellor of Acadia University.

■ **Helen Creighton** (1899–1989) was a song collector, folklorist, and writer from Dartmouth. She worked with the National Museum of Canada and the U.S. Library of Congress to publish more than 4,000 songs in English, French, Gaelic, Micmac, and German.

6 **Samuel Cunard** (1797–1865), born in Halifax, founded one of the first shipping businesses to use steamships. His ships routed mail between England, Nova Scotia, Québec, and Massachusetts. In 1878 this company became the Cunard Line, which carried passengers on huge superliners across the Atlantic Ocean from New York to Europe.

7 **Abraham Gesner** (1791–1864), a geologist, chemist, and inventor, has been called the founder of the modern petroleum industry. He perfected a lamp oil that he called kerosene and invented asphalt paving. Gesner was born in Cornwallis, Nova Scotia.

8 **Thomas Chandler Haliburton** (1796–1865) was an author, judge, and politician who coined such phrases as "raining cats and dogs" and "barking up the wrong tree." Born in Windsor, Nova Scotia, Haliburton was also a member of the provincial legislature and a judge on the Supreme Court of Nova Scotia.

■ **Rita Joe** (born 1935) is a writer from Eskasoni, a Micmac reserve in Nova Scotia. Through her poems and stories, which include children's books, Joe has worked to preserve the language and culture of the Micmacs.

10 **Anna Leonowens** (1834–1915), born in Wales, was an author and teacher who moved to Halifax in 1876. She wrote two books about her travels to Siam (now Thailand), which were the basis for the 1951 play *The King and I.* Leonowens also helped found what is now the Nova Scotia College of Art and Design.

■ **Bryden MacDonald** (born 1962) is a playwright and director. His plays, which include *Whale Riding Weather* and *Weekend Healer,* usually deal with social issues. MacDonald is from Halifax.

12 **Rita MacNeil** (born 1944) is a singer known for her wide range of styles, including folk, country, Celtic, blues, and rock. Her last seven albums, including *Thinking of You* and *Once Upon a Christmas,* have each sold more than 100,000 copies. MacNeil is from Big Pond, Nova Scotia.

61

13 **Robert MacNeil** (born 1931), a journalist from Halifax, worked for the U.S. broadcasting network NBC as a London correspondent beginning in 1960. In 1975 he developed a news show for the U.S. public television network PBS, which became the *MacNeil/Lehrer News Hour*. MacNeil retired from the show in 1995.

■ **Donald Marshall, Jr.** (born 1953), from Sydney, was wrongly convicted of murder in 1972. Sentenced to life in prison, Marshall served 11 years before he was proven innocent. Marshall's struggle brought nationwide attention to the case and encouraged leaders to reexamine Nova Scotia's justice system.

15 **Ian McKinnon** (born 1963), a bagpiper and member of the musical group Rawlins Cross, is from Halifax. In 1991 he started the company Ground Swell Records, which distributes records by Atlantic Canadians to stores all over Canada.

16 **Sarah McLachlan** (born 1968) is a singer and songwriter from Halifax. Her soulful lyrics and moody, folk style have made her a top artist in both Canada and the United States. Her albums include *Touch, Solace,* and *Fumbling Toward Ecstasy.*

17 **Anne Murray** (born 1945) is a pop and country singer who has sold more than 20 million albums worldwide. Her hits include "Snowbird," "I Just Fall in Love Again," and "Daydream Believer." Murray is from Springhill, Nova Scotia.

18 Dan Paul (born 1939) is a human rights activist, lecturer, and author. Born on a Micmac reserve near Shubenacadie, Nova Scotia, he worked for the Canadian Department of Indian Affairs and headed the Confederacy of Mainland Micmacs. In 1994 Paul became the first Micmac in Nova Scotia to be appointed as a justice of the peace.

19 Evelyn Richardson (1902–1976) was an author from Barrington, Nova Scotia. Her first book, *We Keep a Light,* described her life as the wife of a lighthouse keeper. Richardson, who won many awards for her work, also wrote radio scripts.

20 Margaret Marshall Saunders (1861–1947) wrote stories and novels about pets. Her first book, *Beautiful Joe,* was published in 1894 and became the first Canadian book to sell more than one million copies. Saunders was born in Milton, Nova Scotia.

21 Frank William Sobey (born 1902), from Lyons Brook, Nova Scotia, ran Sobey Stores, a chain of supermarkets. As Sobey's fortune increased, he branched out into other industries, including oil and insurance. For his efforts in bringing industry to the province, Sobey was inducted into the Canadian Business Hall of Fame in 1984.

22 Hank Snow (born 1914) is considered one of the fathers of Canadian country music. His hit song "I'm Movin' On" made him a top country star of the 1950s. Born in Liverpool, Nova Scotia, Snow now lives in Nashville, Tennessee, where he performs at the Grand Ole Opry almost every week.

Maxine Tynes (born 1949) is a poet and teacher from Dartmouth. Her books of poetry, which include *Borrowed Beauty* and *Woman Talking Woman,* reflect her life as a black woman and a feminist. Tynes is the first black person to be appointed to the Board of Governors at Dalhousie University.

Fast Facts

Provincial Symbols

Motto: *Munit Haec et Altera Vincit*
(One defends and the other conquers)
Nickname: Land of Evangeline
Song: "Farewell to Nova Scotia"
Flower: mayflower
Tree: red spruce
Gem: agate
Tartan: blue for the sea and sky, dark and light green for the evergreens and deciduous trees, white for the rocks and coastline surf, gold for the province's Royal Charter, and red for the lion on the province's crest.

Provincial Highlights

Landmarks: Bluenose II based in Halifax Harbor, The Wile Carding Mill in Bridgewater, Fort Anne at Annapolis Royal, Cape Breton Highlands National Park near Chéticamp, Miner's Museum in Springhill, Fortress of Louisbourg in Louisbourg, Citadel National Historic Park in Halifax, Shubenacadie Provincial Wildlife Park in Shubenacadie, Alexander Graham Bell National Historic Site in Baddeck

Annual events: Annapolis Valley Apple Blossom Festival (May), Cabot Pageant in Cape North (June), Mahone Bay Wooden Boat Festival (July), Nova Scotia International Tattoo in Halifax (July), Chapel Island Indian Mission in Chapel Island (July), Acadian Festival in Claire (July), Rockhound Round-Up in Parrsboro (August), Oktoberfest in Lunenburg (October)

Population

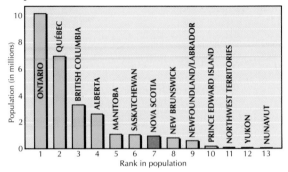

Population*: 900,000
Rank in population, nationwide: 7th
Population distribution: 54 percent urban; 46 percent rural
Population density: 44.1 people per sq mi (17 per sq km)
Capital: Halifax (114,455)
Major cities and towns (and populations*):
Dartmouth (67,798), Sydney (26,552), Glace Bay (19,501), Truro (11,683), Bedford (11,618), New Glasgow (9,905), Amherst (9,742)
Major ethnic groups*: multiple backgrounds, 45 percent; British, 44 percent; French, 6 percent; German, 3 percent; Dutch, 1 percent; North American Indian, Métis, Inuit, 1 percent total

*1991 census

Endangered Species

Mammals: eastern cougar
Birds: harlequin duck, anatum peregrine falcon, piping plover
Fish: Acadian whitefish
Plants: pink coreopsis, eastern mountain avens, thread-leaved sundew, water-pennywort

Geographic Highlights

Area (land/water): 21,425 sq mi (55,490 sq km)
Rank in area, nationwide: 12th
Highest point: North Barren Mountain (1,747 ft/532 m)
Major lakes and rivers: Bras d'Or Lake, Lake Rossignol, Annapolis River, La Have River, Mersey River, Saint Mary's River, Shubenacadie River

Average Temperatures

January: 23F / -5C
July: 64F / 18C

Economy

Percentage of Workers Per Job Sector:

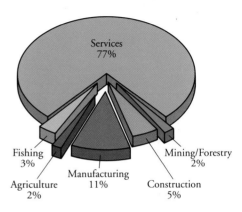

Services 77%
Fishing 3%
Agriculture 2%
Manufacturing 11%
Construction 5%
Mining/Forestry 2%

Natural resources: forests, fertile soil, gypsum, coal, natural gas, oil, barite, clay, gold, limestone, salt, sand and gravel, zinc
Agricultural products: beef and dairy cattle, chickens, eggs, hogs, blueberries, apples, potatoes, strawberries, tobacco, mink farms, Christmas trees
Manufactured goods: food and beverage processing, fish products, dairy products, preserved fruits, paper products, tires, transportation equipment, wood products, petroleum products, steel

Energy

Electric power: coal and oil (85 percent), hydroelectric (15 percent)

65

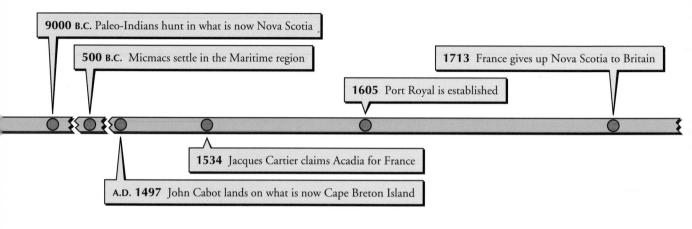

9000 B.C. Paleo-Indians hunt in what is now Nova Scotia

500 B.C. Micmacs settle in the Maritime region

1713 France gives up Nova Scotia to Britain

1605 Port Royal is established

1534 Jacques Cartier claims Acadia for France

A.D. 1497 John Cabot lands on what is now Cape Breton Island

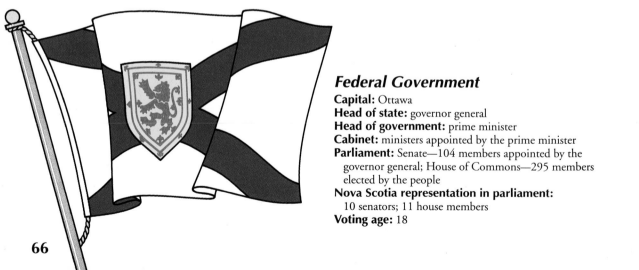

Federal Government

Capital: Ottawa
Head of state: governor general
Head of government: prime minister
Cabinet: ministers appointed by the prime minister
Parliament: Senate—104 members appointed by the
   governor general; House of Commons—295 members
   elected by the people
Nova Scotia representation in parliament:
   10 senators; 11 house members
Voting age: 18

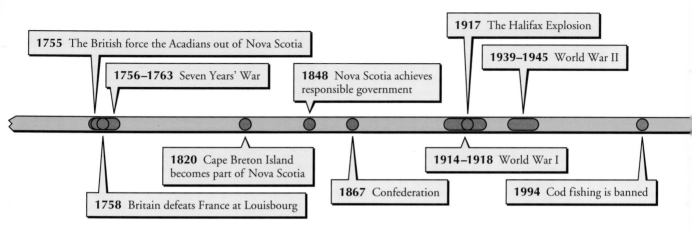

1755 The British force the Acadians out of Nova Scotia

1756–1763 Seven Years' War

1848 Nova Scotia achieves responsible government

1917 The Halifax Explosion

1939–1945 World War II

1820 Cape Breton Island becomes part of Nova Scotia

1758 Britain defeats France at Louisbourg

1867 Confederation

1914–1918 World War I

1994 Cod fishing is banned

Provincial Government

Capital: Halifax
Head of state: lieutenant-governor
Head of government: premier
Cabinet: ministers appointed by the premier
Legislative Assembly: 52 members elected to terms that can last up to five years
Voting age: 18
Major political parties: Liberal and Progressive Conservative

Government Services

To help pay the people who work for Nova Scotia's government, Nova Scotians pay taxes on money they earn and on many of the items they buy. The services run by the provincial government assure Nova Scotians of a high quality of life. Government funds pay for medical care, for education, for road building and repairs, and for facilities such as libraries and parks. In addition, the government has funds to help people who are disabled, elderly, or poor.

Glossary

causeway   A thick wall usually built over wet land or water to serve as a bridge. Cars, trains, and other vehicles can travel across the top of the causeway.

colony   A territory ruled by a country some distance away.

Confederation   The union of four British colonies under the British North America Act in 1867. Confederation formed the Dominion of Canada and set up two levels of government—national and provincial. Other provinces later joined the original four.

dike   A wall or dam built to keep a sea or a river from overflowing.

glacier   A large body of ice and snow that moves slowly over land.

immigrant   A person who moves into a foreign country and settles there.

Loyalist   A person who supports the government during a revolt.

marsh   A spongy wetland soaked with water for long periods of time. Marshes are usually treeless. Grasses are the main form of vegetation found in marshes.

peninsula   A stretch of land almost completely surrounded by water.

primary resource   A raw material, such as a tree or a mineral, that can be processed into a manufactured product.

reserve   Public land set aside by the government to be used by Native peoples.

responsible government A form of government that made the governor responsible (answerable) to an assembly elected by the people.

sanctuary A place where birds and animals are protected from hunters.

tartan A plaid pattern with stripes of different widths and colors originally worn by the Scots. Each clan, or group of families, has its own pattern.

Pronunciation Guide

Acadia (uh-KAY-dee-uh)

Annapolis Royal (uh-NA-puh-luhs ROY-ahl)

Bras d'Or (BRA DAWR)

Cape Breton (KAYP BREHT-uhn)

Cartier, Jacques (kahr-tee-AY, ZHAHK)

Champlain, Samuel de (shaw^n-PLA^n, sah-myoo-EHL duh)

Cobequid (KAHB-uh-KWIHD)

Dartmouth (DAHRT-muhth)

La Have (luh HAYV)

Monts, Pierre du Gua de (MOH^n, pee-EHR doo GAH duh)

Shubenacadie (SHOO-behn-ah-cah-dee)

Index

About the Author

Alexa Thompson is a writer, editor, and educational consultant whose projects include early reader books for children. She also edits *Celtic Heritage,* an international magazine for people of Scottish, Irish, Welsh, or Cornish ancestry. Thompson lives with her husband and two sons in Halifax, Nova Scotia.

Acknowledgments

Mapping Specialists Ltd., pp. 1, 12–13, 46; Voscar, The Maine Photographer, pp. 2, 7, 9, 10, 11 (right), 19 (top), 44, 49; Artwork by Terry Boles, pp. 6, 12, 46, 65; Tourism Nova Scotia, pp. 8, 18, 50, 51 (left), 52, 53 (left), 55, 56 (left and right), 57, 58 (left), 59, 71; David Thompson, Halifax, pp. 11 (left), 19 (bottom), 20, 38, 40, 43, 53 (right), 69, 70; Department of Fisheries and Oceans, Communications Branch, Halifax, p. 15; © James P. Rowan, pp. 16, 41; Jim Simondet, p. 17; Jerry Hennen, pp. 21, 22–23; Nova Scotia Museum, p. 25; Confederation Life Gallery of Canadian History, p. 26; Claude Picard, Artist/Commissioned by Canadian Heritage (Parks Canada), Atlantic Region, pp. 29 (detail), 31 (detail); Lewis Parker, Artist/Parks Canada, Fortress of Louisbourg National Historic Site, p. 30; National Archives of Canada, p. 33 (C168), 35 (C22002), 36 (PA53514), 37 (C3625), 60 (bottom left, C7044), 61 (top left, C6087); Artwork by John Erste, p. 45; Nova Scotia Power Corporation, p. 47; Tourism Halifax, p. 48; Industry, Science, and Technology Photo, pp. 51 (right), 54, 58 (right); Edward Gajdel, p. 60 (top right); Alex Colville, p. 60 (bottom right); Public Archives of Nova Scotia, pp. 34, 60 (middle left), 61 (top right), 61 (middle right), 63 (top right), 63 (middle left); Mark Mainguy, p. 61 (bottom left), 62 (bottom right); MacNeil/Lehrer Productions, p. 62 (top right); Netwerk Productions, p. 62 (middle left); Carol Kennedy/Ground Swell Productions, p. 62 (middle right); Dan Paul, p. 63 (top left); The Sobey Foundation, Stellarton, Nova Scotia, p. 63 (middle right); The Hank Snow Collection, p. 63 (bottom left).